Jogging *with the* Great Ray Charles

ALSO BY KENNETH SHERMAN

POEMS

Black River
The Well: New and Selected Poems
Clusters
Open to Currents
Jackson's Point
The Book of Salt
Relations: Family Portraits, ed.
Black Flamingo
Words for Elephant Man
The Cost of Living
Snake Music

PROSE

Wait Time: A Memoir of Cancer
What the Furies Bring
Void and Voice: Essays on Literary and Historical Currents

Jogging *with the* Great Ray Charles

Kenneth Sherman

a misFit book

Published by ECW Press
665 Gerrard Street East
Toronto, Ontario, Canada, M4M 1Y2
416-694-3348 / info@ecwpress.com

Get the eBook free!*
*proof of purchase required

Purchase the print edition
and receive the eBook free!
For details, go to ecwpress.com/eBook.

Editor for the press:
Michael Holmes/a misFit book
Cover design: Rachel Ironstone
Cover photo: Rich Niewiroski Jr.
"Our Home" (p.39) and "My Friend Is Dying" (p.40) translated from the Yiddish of Simcha Simchovitch by permission.

LIBRARY AND ARCHIVES CANADA
CATALOGUING IN PUBLICATION

Sherman, Kenneth, 1950–, author
Jogging with the great Ray Charles / Kenneth Sherman.

Poems.
Issued in print and electronic formats.
ISBN 978-1-77041-344-3 (paperback)
ALSO ISSUED AS: 978-1-77090-942-7 (PDF)
978-1-77090-941-0 (ePUB)

I. Title.

PS8587.H3863J64 2016 C811'.54 C2016-902321-4
C2016-902322-2

The publication of *Jogging with the Great Ray Charles* has been generously supported by the Canada Council for the Arts, which last year invested $153 million to bring the arts to Canadians throughout the country, and by the Government of Canada through the Canada Book Fund. *Nous remercions le Conseil des arts du Canada de son soutien. L'an dernier, le Conseil a investi 153 millions de dollars pour mettre de l'art dans la vie des Canadiennes et des Canadiens de tout le pays. Ce livre est financé en partie par le gouvernement du Canada.* We also acknowledge the support of the Ontario Arts Council (OAC), an agency of the Government of Ontario, which last year funded 1,737 individual artists and 1,095 organizations in 223 communities across Ontario for a total of $52.1 million, and the contribution of the Government of Ontario through the Ontario Book Publishing Tax Credit and the Ontario Media Development Corporation.

PRINTED AND BOUND IN CANADA

PRINTING: COACH HOUSE PRINTING 5 4 3 2 1

IN MEMORY OF HAROLD HEFT

ONE

CLARINET

Ebony body that flared to a bell.
Tone holes and cool reflecting keys.
The reed of Ishtar
resonating in the humid chamber.
Sobs of klezmer on the banks
of the Vistula, or swelling symphonic
in the court of some Frederick.
O little Claire —
my splayed fingers manoeuvred.

Months of wrenching squeaks
until that first clear note
opened a smile on the face of Mr. Hargreaves,
our school conductor
(embouchure, timbre, slurs),
and I ran home to uncover
my father's stack of 78s:
the silky cadence of Artie Shaw,
the mongrel tremolo of Sidney Bechet.

Orphic stick, moody tube, please forgive me:
in 1966 I put you to rest in your plush
velvet case, took up the electric guitar
to be one of the rockers.
Now you're down in the basement
with all things left off, not carried through,
though I imagine a second life
where the promise of your higher register
is kept and your whole note lingers.

TRANSISTOR RADIO

Cool blue, rectangular,
held to the ear
it gave off the doo-wop,
the backup, the echo and soul,
the hip-grind and throb
of the Monkey, Mashed Potato.

An infinitesimal
turn of the dial
poured out the forecasts, traffic,
Jungle Jay's shtick,
talk show dementia,
requests out to Sue and to Rick.

Giveaways, getaways,
flux of the age.
The jangle, the jingles —
our right to blare.
Those crackling voices
dissolved into air.

JOGGING WITH THE GREAT RAY CHARLES

What I feel is old jogger's happiness
running along the salt-stained boardwalk
within earshot of surf.
Warmed tendons, loosened limbs,
the blessed rhythm of my steady breathing.
And I'm helped along by the iPod clarity of Ray.
Now there's a voice to stand time's test.
Some blues grind harsh,
the soul strung out along six stark strings
or straining hard through the reeds
of a keening harp, but Ray's — complete
with backup brass and chorus — can uplift.
I too have drowned in my own tears,
but not today. Today gulls drift,
cacti shine, tropical fronds fan out
like fishes' vertebrae. All around
sand is common though precious,
glinting along morning's diamond-crusted edge.
I pad beneath sun's benediction,
hit now and then by a fine salt spray
that keeps me focused in the present tense.
I'm in sync with Ray's upbeat
and don't even mind the younger and quicker
who pass me in their latest gear
then speed out of reach. Notes last
while these bodies flashing by —
the bright, the ecstatic —
sooner or later vanish.
We sing, man. Then we're gone.

CONTRA LANGUAGE

Language, unlike music, is condemned to have meaning.
It carries the reproachable human need to explain,

to justify, to convince, and, ultimately, to plead.
To ask forgiveness. It can never know

the simple joy of a clarinet, the self-delighting
ripple of a trumpet, the surge of a keyboard,

or the unpretentious rhythm of a drum.
Words, no matter what their tempo,

are slowed to a hobble by thought.
They must drag the weight of their double lives

through the mental gate
before entering the body.

Music goes directly, while words
are our unique and devious invention

providing a fair approximation of our dust-bound being
that wishes nothing more than to dance. To sing.

BERLIOZ

Alack! my child is dead;
And with my child my joys are buried.
— Capulet

It was quite a concert, our city's youth orchestra
performing Hector Berlioz's *Romeo and Juliet.*
Between the crescendos
I could hear Tybalt curse and Juliet sigh.
I could hear Friar Laurence
recommend the vial of magic potion.
I could hear Romeo's footsteps
as he rushed toward the crypt
and I knew that no matter how furiously
the young violinists sawed away at their instruments
nothing would save the doomed lovers.
What inspired such music?
The first time young Berlioz saw Shakespeare's tragedy
he fell head over heels for the actress playing Juliet.
Her name was Harriet Smithson
and Berlioz's parents despised her,
called her "a penniless Protestant."
Berlioz persisted with love letters, flowers,
chocolates. The marriage didn't last.
Harriet began to drink, forgot her lines,
stumbled onstage, blamed her failing acting career
on her husband's success.
And that was not the end of their sadness.
They had one child, Louis,
who became a merchant sea captain.
At thirty-three he contracted yellow fever
and died aboard his ship, headed for the tropics.

When Berlioz heard the news,
he said he could feel the insufferable heat,
the nauseating sway of the boat.
He grew inconsolable,
burned all his correspondence,
sold everything he possessed, everything
except a baton given to him by Mendelssohn,
one dark suit in which he could continue to conduct
and in which he could be decently buried,
and a doleful guitar —
a gift from Paganini.

HEART

So there you are at last,
on the diagnostician's screen,
fluctuating between clinical grey
and amber, chambers
opening and closing:
a mollusc
kneading its vital fluid.

You look so primitive.
Who would suspect you to inhabit
a human chest, to fasten
with such tenacity
onto memories, lyrics,
frames of an old black-
and-white film?

Hoarder, I lie awake at night
hearing you *thump thump*
as if you were banging on the door
of my life, pleading
for one more chance
to wipe the slate clean
and begin again.

AWAITING BIOPSY RESULTS

"Suffering," says Simone Weil,
"is time without direction."
Light cuts through the blinds
razor thin. In your state
of suspended animation
you listen for your heart
to beat
for the phone
to ring
for a voice
to call you back
to the living.

A DREAM OF LEAVING THE TORONTO GENERAL

I arose from my hospital bed
dressed and walked out of my room
and down the corridor

the nurses did not recognize me
I knew I was the colour of a cadaver

in the elevator I stared straight ahead
avoiding the eyes of the orderlies

I walked into the street
and joined the press of people
going their determined ways

it was a comfort to have a direction
my illness had made me desultory
I had been riding death's wave
and now I was once again like
everyone
like everyone I strode with the swell
of human traffic
anxious over things
that needed doing

I reached the corner
and fixed eyes with a street singer
I knew no one in life has eyes
that intense that focused
his mouth moved soundless
he strummed silence on his guitar
his plush-lined case
swung open like a coffin

and for a moment I panicked
believing I'd been walking
through the land
of the living dead

I tossed him a coin and kept walking
blending with the crowd
hoping that he could not see
the mark upon me

VENUS OCCLUDED

I awoke one morning to discover one eye
weird, blurry, as if opened underwater.
At first I thought I was imagining the effect,
denial my reaction to any physical mishap.
But two days later I found myself sitting
in the darkened chamber, the ophthalmologist
hunched over me, his miner's light probing
the flooded landscape of my retina. "There it is."
Then the ominous pause. "A venous occlusion . . .
some damage . . ." I understood occlusion as blockage,
but not being from the scientific side of things
or wanting, perhaps, to accept responsibility for failed vision,
I heard him speak the name of the goddess
and wondered if those images were fading
because they'd not been loved enough.

PREDICTABLE

They say things are never worse than one
imagines, but that is not true.

For instance, history, general or personal,
is not predictable.

Who could have foretold the stupidity
of the Somme, or the orderliness

of Auschwitz? Who could have forecast
the dissolution of your marriage,

the suddenness of your disease? What's true
is that there is an end to even the worst

suffering. It comes to rest in that place
where there is no more expectation.

There, dark reflects dark
on night's moonless horizon.

You lie perfectly still. The only
business at hand is your decomposition

carried out by laws of the mineral world
that are slow and fairly predictable.

UMBRELLA

It smells of the molten metropolis,
of asphalt and tar,

and folds into the palm of my hand
compact as a bat, silent, aware,

ready to open like a judicial robe
against the rage of unexpected weather.

Thin as my skin and like my skin
it remembers downpour, drizzle,

drops that build slowly as tears (words
grow stale but tears are always fresh).

Dark canopy
to shield against sky's darkness.

TWO

YOU

It's your birthday.

Make some sacrifice
to the god of possible
fireworks
so that when you die
your spirit does not
go soggy.

Stay bright and crisp
in the waiting ear
listening
for your door to open
onto a sky
that permits you
to fly
in dreams.

Do not abandon yourself
to the larvae
of the unfulfilled.

Do not rummage among
old leaves
of your personal history
unless you have found
a way
to set them ablaze.

The genius of any house
walks in a direction
other than what
is given.

WESTERN

I went up to take a nap.
Once I closed my eyes
horses were running out of Texas,
big-eyed schizoid gallopers
and their riders: wild, unshaven men,
the broad brims of their hats blown back.
They were riding through a storm
and I was riding with them. I tell you
I hardly ever dream, I seldom travel, and there I was
past Devils Elbow and Dry Gulch, following a lead.
What were we chasing — Gold? A thief?
I asked but no one heard my voice above the thunder.
I thought the galloping would never end, but
then, in a flash, I was back on my avenue,
its measured lampposts and tight curbs.
Someone was digging. I could hear
the solitary scrape of a shovel,
but when I asked whose funeral,
no one would answer. They motioned me
to take off my hat and we sang a hymn.
I can't recall the words, though I do remember
the gaping hole flooded with late-day light,
and how I turned suddenly to see my horse stomping,
impatient for me to ride.

NORTH

What if I had been born elsewhere,
far from these wasted barns and barren fields,
far from these leafless, white-boned birches
that persist under a shrouded sun?

What if I had been born
where neighbours share balconies,
and down in the street everyone flows with the drums,
the masks, the fireworks of some crazed politics?

Then I wouldn't need you to scrutinize
my tracks in snow or decipher my icy silences.
I'd strum a vulnerable guitar
and open my heart so that you'd think of me

as your *hombre dulce*, a red gardenia pinned
to my white lapel. Charms, spells, the scent
of eucalyptus. Not these spaces between us.
Not these glazed roads that say treacherous.

TO MY BROTHER

Go ahead, dear brother, and carry on the
family tradition that I have sadly broken
by dabbling in words. Speak to me of

interest rates, percentages, and second mortgages.
Tell me the details of your latest real estate
deal so I can envisage that disused factory

in a dead part of our city swept clean
and refashioned by you into a hive of lofts —
lights burning into the night —

its tenants coming and going
rich with possibilities. I, whose
mind goes numb once numbers are spoken,

whose head gets dizzy staring at a bank
statement, regard you in utter amazement.
In my world two plus two rarely equals

four and risk involves groping toward
what only seems, while you embrace
the irrefutable solidity of money.

I wish my pockets jangled like yours.
I wish my wallet closed and opened
like a mouth that knew what fed it.

HOW TO PREVENT YOUR OWN CONCEPTION

Start by turning off the radio.
No point in having the two of them
listening to Peggy Lee's "Fever."

Next, substitute a plate of plain pasta
for the raw, provocative oysters
they are about to swallow

then perform a reverse miracle
by turning their glasses of wine
into water. If at all possible,

push the red hands of the kitchen clock
ahead to midnight
so that they feel too tired to dance.

How sweet it will be to watch them
yawn and nod off
without so much as a whisper.

Now if he happens to get hard as a gun
it will safely go off
in his dreams.

Let the two of them grope and pant
on another night, spinning out
a different set of chromosomes

so that you may spend eternity
in this graceful state of pre-existence,
watching from a distance

the weird antics of those two
and silently commiserating
with their slightly deranged offspring.

THE COLLECTOR

I began at seven
with stones I stored in a plastic container:
some were smooth and dark grey,
others dazzled with splinters

of quartz. Then it was marbles
that bulged in a bag of blue velvet
soft as my grandmother's skin.
Swirls and cat's eyes. Some too precious

to roll along the rough schoolyard pavement.
And baseball cards I loved for the smell
of the gum and the comical sketch on the back
that showed balls flying pell-mell

off a slugger's bat. What envy I felt
when some kid flashed his Topps Mickey Mantle
as if my owning that would — what? —
make me immortal.

Though I wouldn't have thought that
back then. No. Then it was matchboxes
from restaurants where my parents dined.
I glued them to bristol board like little flags:

Barberian's Steak House (red letters on black),
Rossini (swirls of Florentine script).
And stamps picturing kings with pointy beards,
physicists, gymnasts, and poets

from countries I found on an outdated map,
place names that long ago vanished.
And books most of all. I'd search the shelves
and surge with excitement

spotting a Canetti or Levi (Carlo
or Primo), then sink disappointed, recalling
I already owned it. It couldn't be added
to that world I'd been building

since first bending down
to pick up one stone, then another.
That world
where there is no end to desire.

REVISION

The development: that's where I grew up
listening to the roar of the Bobcat
as it gouged fresh foundations
for rows of split-level houses.

The trowel's scrape of cement
and the dull repetitive stroke of the hammer
echoing in the grey autumn air.

What was there to do but shut my bedroom door
and read Camus? *The Stranger* fed my bourgeoning
ennui. How I longed to be as detached and stoical
as the existential criminal Meursault.
He showed no remorse and never flinched,
not even when he focused on the blade of the waiting
guillotine, not even when he stared into the cosmic abyss.

I recall turning the final page of the novel
and rising from my bed,
feeling as though something inside me had shifted.
Cold and superior, I stared steely-eyed out my window
at the impenetrable sky, at the meaningless swirl of stars,
and at the vacant, not-yet-sold house across the road with its
newly installed windows. It was waiting to be inhabited
by the bourgeoisie, those we-in-the-know called "the living dead."

Attitude for an adolescent. One goes into the world
and finds there are few Meursaults.
For most of us it's fears and longings.

Tonight, I stare across the road
and see, in the house opposite mine, someone staring back.
A sharp blade would frighten either one of us.

ON FIRST READING *HAMLET*

After all these years
a few core scenes reveal themselves through time's mist:
mother lying in bed depressed and mostly speechless, and me,
during that, to put it mildly, unsettling month, discovering
the dead king's mission-bound hoary ghost clanking his armour
over the damp turrets and ramparts in search of a son's ear.
Why should the ghost of another man's father have spoken to me?
And other mysteries: her tirades and punitive silences,
the origins of which I will never know.
I like to think they've receded into the past,
diminishing with age,
though the difficult truth is they cling,
erupting now and then into enraged flares of disharmony
and light. The dew upon the brow of the young prince
bidding his father *adieu* and wishing more than anything
that he would stay
and speak a moment longer.

THE TAILOR

On a frigid January night
when all that lives
is scurrying for shelter,
I imagine him in the deep shadows
following me home.

The sky's a bolt of silk.
The moon, a dented thimble.
The stars, spilt pins.

His quick steps on the icy pavement
are the clacking of a sewing machine.
Even in death there are
things that need taking care of.

One night I expect him to spring
from the darkness
clutching a page from the book of my life
as if it were an unpaid statement.

What can I say to calm him
so that the two of us
might carry on?

THE HOME

This is the home where the crime was committed,
where the rebellion was put down,
where voices rose higher than flames
and where now there is no sound.

The children have left. In their various
heads the battles rage on. Their hands
commit deeds they say they never intended,
and they weep or stand dumbfounded.

Days proliferate with a sameness
and sequence that takes them back
to the family den where two figures sit
malignant in shadow and unjustly potent.

AT THE GLENDALE THEATRE, 1957

A mere quarter got you in.
At first it was twilit pandemonium:
whistling, wisecracks,
popcorn tossed at your neighbour's head
until darkness fell, the trailers rolled,
and that woman in white
began to patrol the aisles,
threatening to freeze you in flashlight.

A lion's roar heralded the feature,
the future. And those titles —
The Day the World Ended. Them!
The entire audience hushed in communion
as a small light streamed from the projectionist's cell,
widening into a world of black and white
where events progressed with the speed of a disease
and eyes on the screen widened in horror.

For ninety minutes you clung to your seat
and then only half-believed
that simple declaration, *The End.*
What a relief it was to step into the afternoon light
with its rush of colours
and to hear, as you made your way home
past familiar lawns and houses,
the precious, unrehearsed voices.

LAYTON

His office, a late light burning
in the grey monolith
of the new university.
Poured concrete, sealed windows.
"An afterthought of Albert Speer," he quipped.

Around his neck he wore an ancient
medallion engraved with the goddess.

He praised the Greek islands, women, ouzo,
but the eyes that scanned your soul
were those of a Talmudist.

He welcomed me,
a neophyte with manuscript in trembling hand,
and read my poems aloud,
making them credible to my ear.

"Don't question your talent.
Can't you see you're blessed
with Jewish anxiety?"

Once, after discussing poetry
and the Holocaust,
he lit a matchbox and together
we sat in silence
watching it flame into nothing
in the ashtray
on his desk.

LITTLE GRANDMOTHER

My little grandmother
in a smeared apron
wire-rimmed spectacles

you died when I was
a child
my image of you blurry
as if seen through
frosted glass

you kept chickens in your yard
that you butchered
and wrapped   sent my mother
a young girl
to carry stinking packages
down Baldwin Street
collecting cold quarters
from customers

you told me nothing
of the pogroms wars
                    your sisters
in cattle cars

you didn't want to deprive me
of childhood
                    turn my happiness
to cinders

your painterly apron's red and yellow
the blood and fat of slaughtered fowls

breasts drumsticks
featherless wings

I recall you saying
the days are long
the years
short

THE WAR

She told me the village from which she came
was so small, if a horse stood on Main
its nose and tail would stick out either end of town.
Still they came and burned the place down.

SALVAGED PAGES

They've been collected, the diaries
and testimonies written by young people
in the months and days
leading up to the camps:

Dad had called Aunt Kate in Berlin who was to pick me up.

I am in bed. Nothing from you though I think of you often.

A girl as pretty as a picture — if she could be shot
then the end of the world will soon be here.

If you read long enough you come upon the
ultimate questions:

If we are good, why this?

If there is a God, why is He silent?

Each teenager
a budding philosopher,
waiting at the station,
suitcase in hand.

A CONTEMPORARY

After his wife left — she wasn't Jewish —
took the kids and took up with — to his mind —
a nogoodnik — he became Lubavitch

and bought himself a Harley-Davidson.
You can see him early summer mornings
after prayers, accentuating the contradictions:

his engine screaming down sleepy streets,
martial helmet and sacred fringes,
denim vest and sweep of patriarchal beard blown back

as if caught in a prophetic wind.

PHOTOGRAPH OF A TALMUDIST

(Taken in Warsaw, 1936)

I will not infer from your black suit
and stiff blanched collar an absolutist's stance
since moot distinctions were your passion,
nor read prophecy into your ashen beard
though your forehead, pale as a candle, burned,
as did the bald dome beneath your silk skullcap.

Your terse lips questioned transcendence,
your magnified eyes pondered the invisible
from behind the flash of spectacles.
Man of substance, you were suspicious
of these captured appearances on paper —
you who inhabited thought and lived stateless.

OUR HOME

Our one-room house is cold and damp,
Lit by a meagre kerosene lamp.
In the centre stands a table, battered,
Two wobbly benches, a half-filled cupboard.
In the makeshift kitchen, mother stands
By the faltering fire, her red chapped hands
Peel stunted carrots, small potatoes.
And there in the corner, cast in shadow,
The sewing machine my father works at,
Day after day, from morning to sunset.
Sometimes it buzzes like a housefly, trapped,
Or hums like a woman, old, demented.
Mother brings thin soup to the table.
She sighs each time she dips the ladle.
After soup, I take my book and retreat
To a world where characters have enough to eat.
Outside I hear the stiff wind blow
Rattling frames and threatening my window.
Asleep, my sisters hold one another
In ascending age, ending with mother.
Father lies down. I hear him cough.
My eyes are fighting heaviness.
I make for my folding cot by the door.
Cold creeps up from the wooden floor
And follows me into my sagging bed.
Our days are bound by the darkest thread.

from the Yiddish of Simcha Simchovitch

MY FRIEND IS DYING

He's huddled in the shade of this towering fence
To escape the raging, blistering sun
And now he's dying — my long-time friend —
Here in a land that is strange and foreign.

We go back to boyhood. Together we dreamed
And planned to do much in our future years
But who can foretell what the days have in store:
Tanks. Bombs. The cold executioners.

We escaped and travelled in constant fear.
We made our way east to Kazakhstan.
Now he curls on the earth and groans in pain.
His sunken face is the mask of a dying old man.

Hunger, like rust, ate at his body. Typhus
Ravaged his youthful frame.
I am fated to look on, desperate, helpless,
And in prayers for the dead, intone his name.

from the Yiddish of Simcha Simchovitch

FOUR QUESTIONS

Why does a dog howl at the moon?
He thinks it's a succulent bone.
Why do stars plummet too soon?
It's tiresome being with God.

Why does a river never cease?
It runs from the sound of nothing.
Why do we clear the land of trees?
So that beasts can come to the city.

from the Yiddish of Leyzer Volf

THREE

NO TRACKS

Snow falling. Children grown and gone.
Rooms have taken on the hush of a museum.
I pass bedrooms where the only lodgers
are wide-eyed dolls and action figures.

There are no tracks outside my window
to guide a traveller through the deepening snow.
I hear the house settle and creak
as if something within still wanted to speak.

CHERRY TOMATOES

The French called them *pommes d'amour*.
To the English they were dangerous —
sister of henbane, mandrake, nightshade,
thought to unbalance the humours
and lead to grave indiscretions.
Yet year after year you planted rows of them,
staked to old broom handles,
bladeless hockey sticks,
and cared for them like a worried parent
with watering and weeding.
Each May, you put down a row of marigolds,
blond hoplites, your first line of defence
against the rapacious slugs and aphids.
Summer's war shrivelled their golden heads
but behind them your delectable survivors
fed by sunlight and the damp underground's
turbulent decay.
Late August, when daylight faded
and shadows perched over the desiccated bed,
I'd watch from the kitchen window
as you crept over the dry stalks
and knelt to pick them,
your fingers dusted with their pollen,
your face so close to their scarlet flesh
it flushed lantern-like against the gloom.
What were you fending off
as you bent like a supplicant?
Sombre autumn? Encroaching winter,
everything silenced?
Try this, you'd say
and press a small globe to my lips

as if it were a remedy,
as if I'd forgotten tart seed heart,
sun storage, aftertaste of earth.

SNAIL

Who would not covet
a house like yours
striped vortex
ridged nugget
zebra helmet
toting a double sex?

Atop tender tentacles
your periscope eyes
swivel and twist
ogling the delectable
petals
and stems.

By secretion
by slick persistence
you inch your one good foot
over the terminal garden
leaving behind
a luminous path.

You must be one of the Elect.
When dark torrents
wash away earwigs aphids —
all frail wings and whisker-legged
specks — I find you sparkling
clinging to a leaf.

FISHING

Have you forgotten how beautiful
they are, the perch, the pike,
the rock and small-mouth bass
corn yellow about the under-fins
deep blue and moss green,
their iridescent scales shining,
their gelid eyes staring out
from bullet-shaped heads
fronting a sleek persistence?

Catch and release them
to know briefly their mystery
to feel their unequivocal pull
and to sense what lives
in the submerged shadows,
weaving between rocks and reeds,
darting along silent avenues
then slowing, inquisitive, nosing
the ribs of a sunken canoe.

Think of how they navigate
our decay and debris, avoiding
the rusted anchors that held too fast,
passing through tenements
of worn-out tires, vacant cans,
invading our dreams
flashing their purple, silver
and gold, perishable rainbows,
our light to follow.

for Bruce Jacobs

CLOUDS

Out of their billowing whiteness
I improvise a sea horse,
an ogre, a mountain so massive
it could stand in the Himalayas,
where clouds, from what I've read,
last longer than here. In this warm
and volatile atmosphere
clouds grow majestic or ominous.
By sunset they dissolve
into candy floss,
harmless pink wisps.
Over my childhood home
they would amass
into a vast metallic sheet
the air underneath smelling of snails
and dead leaves. They
thundered through the night,
raining down zigzags of light
that scared me half to death.
By morning they vanished
and people said approvingly,
"Not a cloud in the sky,"
as if it were a sign from heaven.
But, really, how long
can you live without them?
How long before you tire
of the grandstanding sun
so bright and predictable,
and impossible to look into.

NORTHERN LAKE

They've given you a name —

Ox-Tongue, Loon Call,
Big Bass, Turtle —

but long before names
you reflected shattered
sun,
                mute clouds,
unconscious eye
of moon.

When the turbulence of wind
pushed you to the limit
you encased yourself in ice
and went silent.

What's nameless in me
goes with you.

You change,
you remain changeless
and these words are nothing more
than a way of making what vanished
permanent

as you lap away at rock
and nourish the deepening cold.

THE MARINA

For me it was the last refuge
between land and deep water,
the final outpost between here
and there. Live bait kept in a fridge:
minnows and blue crayfish,
leeches stretching like snippets
of black elastic, dew worms winding
through buckets of moss.

I'd marvel at the dysfunctional outboard motors
hoisted on wooden saddles,
the exposed mechanisms of carburetors and gears,
and lean down to watch gasoline rainbows
widen on water — violets, emeralds, pinks —
never giving a thought to toxicity
but conjuring in my mind
a dragonfly's iridescent wings.

In the coveted slips of the rich
I'd grin at the cheesy monikers
stencilled on glossy cabin cruisers:
Seize the Bay, *Out to Launch*,
Grim Reefer.

                    I would like to return
though at this age I'd have to take my place
among the chorus of elders. There I am,
wearing a hat pierced with fishing flies,
theorizing about feeding habits, offering advice
on rattle traps, cranks and jigs, attempting to put
a forced, determining spin on fickle-faced luck.

DUSTY

A rural road.
And here comes Henderson
in his rickety wagon
pulled by the indefatigable Dusty.

A heave-ho
and I'm up on the seat,
a set of gullible ears
for the milkman's jabbering.

The thing is, I can't recall
a single one of Henderson's tall tales
though I've retained a close-up view
of his grey stubble,

his veined, sunburned nose
and the worn cowhide reins
he held in his
liver-spotted hands.

I see Dusty's blinkers
and tarnished harness,
her tail switching at morning flies
and note that none of this

was ever filmed or photographed
or put online, but imprinted itself
on my deepest folds, to what purpose
my aging self now speculates.

I hear the *clop clop*
of an old horse's shoes
and the *clink* of fresh bottles
jostling in their crates.

WRINGER-WASHER

It stood in the shed behind our cottage,
solid, unbudgeable, iceberg white,
countering every sign of disuse: torn nets,
old handsaws, reels of tangled line.
Empty, it echoed with the vacancy of metal,
with the forlorn redundancy of inner space.
Working, it hummed with a purposeful
churning, gears and ball bearings,
a joyous swish that came to its end
with a groan of sad parting: its residue —
bubbles of breakable blue.
Shirts, shorts, jeans, and jerseys,
each fed through the mangle,
came out flat and comical —
cartoon coyote pressed by a steamroller.
Long ago it was hauled to the desolate junkyard,
scrap metal iota, dissected for parts,
then crushed and refigured, part of whatever.
Now it returns with the scent of old cedar,
with the fragrance of sheets snapped by wind.
The pure appliance once taken for granted.
Whiteness waiting in the shade of the shed.

PENHALE'S SCHOONER

On a cruise ship, the motion of the sea
converts to a gentle pulse, a cradle sway
that lulls you off to sleep. Nothing like that time
I crewed on Penhale's schooner
when whistling gusts drove out the sails
and the palm-blistering strain of the sheets
brought me to the point of frantic prayer.
Each drop from a swell was a nosedive off a wall.
It went on all day and well into darkness until
the wheel froze and the rudder stuck stiff.
Through the whole of it I recall looking up only once
to see the moon burn white through night's cirrus clouds
moving fast across a sky blacked out and senseless.

THE SEVILLE

Old seaside hotel, derelict,
your rusted railings bake in the heat
and when it rains a putrid orange
trickles down white walls
staining your cracked patio.

When I consider your fractured shutters
and smeared windows
gaping gloomily at the sea,
a sadness overcomes me.
I imagine you dream of new balustrades,
balconies, blinds,
a refurbished sign
to welcome expectant guests.

I have to remind myself you're inanimate,
can't possibly mind the rude graffiti
sprayed on your peeling portico,
the camouflaged lizards
darting guerrilla-like
through your weed-carpeted pool.

Ghost hovel, ruined temple whose elevators
once smelled of lotion and cologne, why do
I find your decrepitude troubling?

I'd prefer a vacant lot
to the thought of your empty halls
and trashed suites

the sound of the wind
scouring
your twilit lobby.

COLÓN, PANAMA

At least the slums are lively: men arguing in the streets,
kids kicking a ball, women balancing baskets of laundry,
radio rhythms of rumba and tango. But the stench and grime
shame you when you step from the tour bus
clutching your digital lens, they have you asking,

Where are those millions earned from the canal?
Unlike water, money in the tropics never trickles down.
It stays frozen at the top. It chills. In the American section
no one's out of doors and a strange silence fills the streets,
emanating from monster houses painted the pink of Disney's castles.

SEASHELLS

Bend to choose one
and you are in the act of supplication.
Shark's eye, lion's paw, Venus clam:
a nomenclature to mute the strangeness
of these primal bits,
tongue's approximation of the deep's deposits,
whorls to the inner ear.

And what do you make with them?
A necklace *par excellence*?
Floridian kitsch?
On my shore the pen shell is ubiquitous,
colour of coal, of shadow, ink sheen
set against blue sea, blue sky.
Not a life but what it leaves behind.

THE VALUE OF REPETITION

Each morning
the same gentle gusts
pass over my restless body.
The surf comes in
as it did before me,
as it will after me.
And the pelicans skim low
over the wide blue gulf.
They've been doing it for ages,
long before a human face
turned toward them
with the realization
that it's difficult to distinguish
one from another:
each has the same oversized,
comical bill, each,
the same ludicrous tuft of hair.
On this shore,
you would have to be a marine biologist
to tell one pen shell from the next,
to differentiate between
all the inert horseshoe crabs.
As for the countless grains of sand —
they're the closest we'll ever get
to the soothing
infinity of things.

GINGKO

Oldest tree on the planet
its branches are not dense.
The leaves have space to breathe
and room to remember.

It has more to remember
than the others, yet its shadow
is not too dark,
not too difficult to bear.

BUDDHA'S PARASOL

A little shade
to protect us
from the heat of longing,
of want.

But who does not want,
who cannot smell
the honey and ginger?

The lime orchard reaches us
even here.

                    Even here
the fragrance of roots
invades.

To be happy like you, Gautama,
smiling
under a portable temple
that mutes the sun

knowing
                    and forgiving

not severe,
                    not wagging a finger.

CONTRA ABSOLUTES

If you do not shine are you darkness?

Think of those grey portraits
taken not at a frail distance
but in crystal close-up, giving pause.

You can exist to considerable effect
between brilliance and the abyss,

a half-lit shadow presence

like the moonstruck maple on your front lawn
rustling its leaves
and seeming to breathe.

HEARING YOUR FAVOURITE POET

The voice is thinner
less resonant
than you expected

something
of a
disappointment

but remember
you don't choose your
voice box

the larynx
grows its own timbre
which may

or may not
be synced
to the soul's hunger.

WISE CRACKS

Vanishing Ink

A phone text is not a letter.
An email does not possess
the density of paper.
Hitting "delete"
is not to crumple or tear.
To hold in the hand
an indictment or a love letter
is heavier than peering
through glass. Electricity
is fast but some things
need to linger, to get lost
in the soul's attic
and be rediscovered.

Scribe

It's a crime
to sit by a pool
while the sun is shining
and your friends
are talking
and you're off in the corner,
pen in hand,
groping for words.
It's slightly inhuman
to record rather than
live,
to act the sieve
collecting each day's

sediment
and passing time
retrospectively —
saying not what you mean
but what you meant.

The Beach, Today, Is Closed

This Portuguese man-of-war
did not wish
to be washed ashore,
but lacking means
to control its direction
found itself wedged
between sea and sand.
Its only hope
is the one Great Wave
whose arrival's
uncertain.
So it waits
and seethes in the sun,
a blue translucent sphere
gathering venom.

Toodle-oo

A cruise ship
sailing into the blue.
Toodle-oo. We don't
say that anymore.

It's an expression
from another age
when people rhymed themselves
to sleep and dreamed
in metaphor.
When blue meant more.

De la Cruz Gallery, Miami

Next to the objects
found in this
installation — the segmented
plumber's pipes and dented
paint cans, the twisted
tortured bicycle wheels
suggesting life is random
fragmented,
nothing
more than material —
there's a large Peter Doig
painting titled "Rainbow
Ferris Wheel." The many-hued
wheel is intact and rendered
with precision
offering a seat for the human
and an alternate view.

Bartender

It's good to watch him work
in white shirt, black
pants, mixing the
spirits, slicing lemons,
limes, shaking a tumbler
close to the ear as though
listening to a whisper.
What hasn't he heard
from the lips of the frustrated,
the forlorn, the obsessed? His
is not to pass judgement
but to pour colours —
burgundy, emerald, amber —
and to stop only
if one stumbles
or slurs.

Obuse, Japan

This is the town
where Hokusai lived
in old age. Everyone recognizes
his "Great Wave"
which, in my book,
is no longer a cliché
but the Nothing
you can drown in.
Legend has it
he would kneel before

this Shinto altar
with the little mirror,
pebbles,
and charred sticks.
Not much to pray to.
Perfect.

FOUR

KINGDOM

1

So the boat sets out
the contractors flee
the storm comes on
and thirty-three men, women
and children risking freedom
go under. I can hear their death chatter.
Voices, what do you say
of the low metallic clouds, the whiplash
wind, the unforgiving turbulence
that refused to cough you up?
Can you describe your new kingdom?

2

I unlace my shoes.
I strap on sandals
and walk along a beach
that appears endless
under a sun that does not quit.
It is so easy in the tropics:
palm trees indifferent
surf hypnotic
shore breeze a soft eraser.
Only geckoes
darting between stones and flora
seem to sense danger.
Little creatures, what do you hear
aside from hip hop at the hotel
aside from poolside splashes
and laughter?

Can you hear the lost ones
whispering over sonar?

3

After thirty seconds
the brain signs off
the heart slams shut
the blood congregates in pools.
The drowned float on the surface
like limp marionettes.
Their skin turns to grave wax
pecked at by small fish.
Their rags bulge with sea slugs —
slimed, curious.

They welter in the parching wind.

Beneath the whirring propellers
of heaven they are anonymous specks,
a radioed position

then a bloating weight
for the winch ropes and pulleys
that haul them up —
a mechanized ascension —

nameless
unclaimed on land.

4

In this place
birds bear no malice
not even when they're scooping fish
or pecking shells for flesh.
Waiters named after angels —
Michael, Gabriel —
dress in white
and black.

Sun drifts off to late sunset
and sky reddens like a stage set
over distant, opalescent islands.

Here there are no
charred prayers
or stained petitions
as darkness descends
and voices soften.

Glasses
rise to lips.
Gin's drowsy kiss.

5

In their country
sand glints like steel
or diamonds
stretching the long length
of the horizon.

In their country
a woman once told an elephant
to stand still,
which is why their trees
stay motionless.
                    Fed by myth,
nourished by earth's
turbulent decay,
they remain rooted.

But the people flee

wounded

burning.

6

The proprietors have clouded my mirror.
They have dimmed the light
in the elevator.
They have made my martini dirty.
To be drunk is to be intimate with a man
practised in the art of forgetting.
Soon it will be a question
of only remembering
how to put my one foot
in front of
the other

of finding
the right
door.

7

Their journey is harder.
Dead but still vulnerable,
they sail by islands
that remain untouchable.

They must weather our breaking currents
careful not to sink
through piles of yellowing newspapers
careful not to pass too quickly
from our pulsing
screens.

They must find a way
to rise above the daily clamour
and have their voices heard

then they must learn to forgive us
our coldness,
                our fleeting
regard.

Acknowledgements are due to the editors of the following publications where earlier versions of some of these poems first appeared: *ARC*, *Ars Medica*, the *Antigonish Review*, *Books in Canada*, the *Canadian Jewish News*, *Canadian Literature*, *Canadian Notes & Queries*, *Contemporary Verse 2*, the *Cortland Review*, the *Danforth Review*, *Exile*, the *Fiddlehead*, *Grain*, the *Jewish Daily Forward* (U.S.), the *Malahat Review*, *Parchment*, *Poetry Quebec*, the *Rotary Dial*, the *Saranac Review* (U.S.), *Stand* (U.K.), *Tikkun* (U.S.), *Vallum*, and the *Warwick Review* (U.K.).

"Photograph of a Talmudist" appeared in the collection *Letters and Pictures from the Old Suitcase* (Pinking Shears Publications).

PHOTO © MARIE SHERMAN

KENNETH SHERMAN has published ten books of poetry, including the highly acclaimed long poems *Words for Elephant Man* and *Black River*. He has published two collections of essays, *Void and Voice* and the award-winning *What the Furies Bring*. His most recent publication is the memoir *Wait Time*. He lives in Toronto, Ontario, where he conducts poetry-writing workshops.